The Music of CHRISTMAS *Plus One*

12 Popular Solos With CD Accompaniments

Arranged by Tony Esposito

Offline production mixed and mastered by John Cameron for britishaudio.com

MW01105047

CONTENTS

ALL I WANT FOR CHRISTMAS IS MY TWO FRONT TEETH

Words and Music by
DAN GOGGIN
Arranged by TONY ESPOSITO

Joyously

CHRISTMAS LULLABY

Music by
CY COLEMAN

Lyrics by PEGGY LEE
Arranged by TONY ESPOSITO

CHRISTMAS MEM'RIES

Words by
ALAN and MARILYN BERGMAN

Music by DON COSTA
Arranged by TONY ESPOSITO

IFM0039CD

CHRISTMAS TIME IS HERE

By LEE MENDELSON
and VINCE GUARALDI
Arranged by TONY ESPOSITO

With lots of feeling

THE CHRISTMAS WALTZ

Words by
SAMMY CAHN

Music by JULE STYNE
Arranged by TONY ESPOSITO

IFM0039CD

I'LL BE HOME FOR CHRISTMAS

Words by
KIM GANNON

Music by WALTER KENT
Arranged by TONY ESPOSITO

Moderately slow

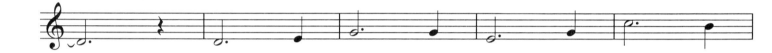

IFM0039CD

HAVE YOURSELF A MERRY LITTLE CHRISTMAS

Words and Music by
HUGH MARTIN and RALPH BLANE
Arranged by TONY ESPOSITO

Ballad style

IT'S THE MOST WONDERFUL
TIME OF THE YEAR

Music and Lyrics by
EDDIE POLA and GEORGE WYLE
Arranged by TONY ESPOSITO

Bright waltz

It's the Most Wonderful Time of the Year - 2 - 1
IFM0039CD

SLEIGH RIDE

Words by
MITCHELL PARISH

Music by LEROY ANDERSON
Arranged by TONY ESPOSITO

IFM0039CD

LET IT SNOW! LET IT SNOW! LET IT SNOW!

Lyric by
SAMMY CAHN

Music by JULE STYNE
Arranged by TONY ESPOSITO

IFM0039CD

THERE IS NO CHRISTMAS LIKE
A HOME CHRISTMAS

Words by
CARL SIGMAN

Music by MICKEY J. ADDY
Arranged by TONY ESPOSITO

WINTER WONDERLAND

Words by
DICK SMITH

Music by FELIX BERNARD
Arranged by TONY ESPOSITO

IFM0039CD